Do Turtles Sleep in Treetops?

A Book About Animal Homes

by Laura Purdie Salas

illustrated by Jeff Yesh

PICTURE WINDOW BOOKS
Minneapolis, Minnesota

Special thanks to our advisers for their expertise:

Zoological Society of San Diego
San Diego Zoo, San Diego, California

Susan Kesselring, M.A., Literacy Educator
Rosemount–Apple Valley–Eagan (Minnesota) School District

Editor: Christianne Jones
Designer: Nathan Gassman
Page Production: Melissa Kes
Creative Director: Keith Griffin
Editorial Director: Carol Jones
The illustrations in this book were created digitally.

Picture Window Books
5115 Excelsior Boulevard
Suite 232
Minneapolis, MN 55416
877-845-8392
www.picturewindowbooks.com

Printed in the United States of America.

Library of Congress Cataloging-in-Publication Data
Salas, Laura Purdie.
Do turtles sleep in treetops? : a book about animal homes / by Laura Purdie Salas ;
illustrated by Jeff Yesh.
p. cm. — (Animals all around)
Includes bibliographical references.
ISBN-13: 978-1-4048-2232-0 (hardcover)
ISBN-10: 1-4048-2232-1 (hardcover)
1. Animals—Habitations—Juvenile literature. I. Yesh, Jeff, 1971- ill. II. Title. III. Series.

QL756.S25 2006
591.56′4—dc22   2006003589

Editor's Note: There is often more than one species of each animal. Unless a specific
species is noted, the homes described in this book are a general overview of what an
animal may build.

Do turtles sleep in treetops?

No! Eagles sleep in treetops.

Bald eagles build huge nests in tall trees. These nests can be 10 feet (3 meters) wide. Eagles use the same nest over and over. They add new sticks, grass, and feathers each year. Sometimes the nest gets so heavy that it breaks the entire tree branch.

Do turtles build wax homes?

No! Bees build wax homes.

Honeybees produce wax, which they use to build their hives. They fill hollow trees with wax honeycomb sheets. Each honeycomb contains many tiny, six-sided cells. The bees put either honey or bee eggs in the cells. Then they seal each cell with more wax.

Do turtles live in underwater dens?

No! An octopus lives in an underwater den.

The Giant Pacific octopus lives in a dark, rocky home. Its soft, squishy body can squeeze through small spaces. Inside its den, the octopus lays more than 50,000 eggs!

Do turtles build lodges?

No! Beavers build lodges.

Beavers use their big front teeth to gnaw down trees. They drag branches and mud into the water to make a lodge. The lodge's entrance is underwater, which helps keep bears, wolves, and other predators out.

Do turtles dig burrows?

No! Prairie dogs dig burrows.

Prairie dogs live in underground burrows connected by tunnels. If a prairie dog spots danger while it's outside its burrow, it dives into the tunnel headfirst. It catches the sides of the tunnel with its legs so it doesn't land on its head.

Do turtles bury themselves in the sand?

No! The sand gaper buries itself in the sand.

The sand gaper is a shellfish that lives below the surface of the sand. The sand keeps the gaper damp and protects it from birds. The gaper stretches a tube, similar to a snorkel, to the surface to breathe. It uses another tube to eat plankton in the sand.

Do turtles create amazing towers?

No! Termites create amazing towers.

Tiny termites build clay homes up to 20 feet (6 m) tall. The towers help termites survive the hot, dry weather. Each tower has many rooms. Some rooms are living rooms. Other rooms are food storage areas.

Do turtles build new nests each day?

No! Chimpanzees build new nests each day.

Chimpanzees live in groups. They eat together and groom each other, but they like to sleep alone. Only a mother and her baby share a nest. At night, each chimpanzee finds a branch 25 to 35 feet (7.6 to 10.7 m) in the air. Each weaves thick branches together with leaves to make a cozy nest.

Do turtles stamp out flat areas to live in?

No! Deer stamp out flat areas to live in.

White-tailed deer stamp out flat spots on the ground where all of the deer huddle together. Each herd lives in a deeryard, which is surrounded by a large area of evergreen trees. During the winter, the trees help block out snow and wind. The deer stay warmer and can more easily find grass and bark to eat in the deeryard.

Do turtles carry their homes on their backs?

Yes! Turtles carry their homes on their backs.

Turtles never have to find or build a home. They grow it right on their bodies. A turtle's shell is made of a bony material. The upper shell covers the turtle's back and sides. The lower shell covers its belly. The turtle's shell protects it from skunks, snakes, and other predators.

Different Animal Homes

Some animals use sticks, leaves, and grass to make a home.

Beavers build lodges of sticks and mud. ·············

 ···· Chimpanzees weave thick branches together with leaves
to make a cozy nest.

Eagles construct nests out of sticks and plants. ··········

Some animals dig down to make a home.

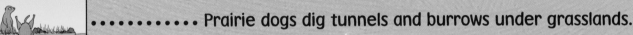

 ············ Prairie dogs dig tunnels and burrows under grasslands.

Sand gapers bury themselves in the sand. ···········

Some animals find homes in nature.

 ············· Deer gather in areas protected by trees.

Octopuses find shelter in rocky dens. ············

Some animals make tall homes.

 ············ Termites build amazing clay towers.

Some animals use their own bodies for homes.

Bees produce wax to make honeycombs. ············

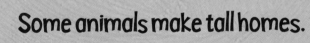 ················Turtles grow their own homes on their backs.

Glossary

evergreen—a plant that stays green all year

honeycomb—a sheet of wax filled with holes

plankton—small plants and animals that float in water

predators—animals that hunt other animals for food

shellfish—an animal that has a shell and lives in or near the water

snorkel—a tube used to let a person breathe underwater

To Learn More

At the Library

Crossingham, John. *What Is Hibernation?* New York: Crabtree Pub., 2002.

Murphy, Patricia J. *Why Do Some Animals Hibernate?* New York: PowerKids Press, 2004.

Perry, Phyllis Jean. *Animals that Hibernate.* New York: Franklin Watts, 2001.

On the Web

FactHound offers a safe, fun way to find Internet sites related to this book. All of the sites on FactHound have been researched by our staff.

1. Visit *www.facthound.com*
2. Type in this special code for age-appropriate sites: 1404822321
3. Click on the FETCH IT button.

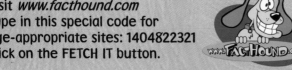

Your trusty FactHound will fetch the best sites for you!

Index

beavers, 10, 23
bees, 6, 23
buried, 13, 14, 23
burrows, 11, 12, 23
chimpanzees, 18, 23
deer, 20, 23
deeryard, 20
eagles, 4, 23
flat areas, 19, 20
lodges, 9, 10, 23
nests, 4, 17, 18, 23
octopus, 8, 23
prairie dogs, 12, 23
sand gaper, 14, 23
termites, 16, 23
towers, 15, 16, 23
treetops, 3, 4
underwater dens, 7, 8, 23
wax homes, 5, 6, 23

Look for all of the books in the Animals All Around series:

Do Bears Buzz? A Book About Animal Sounds
    1-4048-0100-6
Do Bees Make Butter? A Book About Things Animals Make
    1-4048-0288-6
Do Cows Eat Cake? A Book About What Animals Eat
    1-4048-0101-4
Do Crocodiles Dance? A Book About Animal Habits
    1-4048-2230-5
Do Dogs Make Dessert? A Book About How Animals Help Humans
    1-4048-0289-4
Do Ducks Live in the Desert? A Book About Where Animals Live
    1-4048-0290-8
Do Frogs Have Fur? A Book About Animal Coats and Coverings
    1-4048-0292-4
Do Goldfish Gallop? A Book About Animal Movement
    1-4048-0105-7
Do Lobsters Leap Waterfalls? A Book About Animal Migration
    1-4048-2234-8
Do Parrots Have Pillows? A Book About Where Animals Sleep
    1-4048-0104-9
Do Pelicans Sip Nectar? A Book About How Animals Eat
    1-4048-2233-X
Do Penguins Have Puppies? A Book About Animal Babies
    1-4048-0102-2
Do Polar Bears Snooze in Hollow trees? A Book About Animal Hibernation
    1-4048-2231-3
Do Salamanders Spit? A Book About How Animals Protect Themselves
    1-4048-0291-6
Do Squirrels Swarm? A Book About Animal Groups
    1-4048-0287-8
Do Turtles Sleep in Treetops? A Book About Animal Homes
    1-4048-2232-1
Do Whales Have Wings? A Book About Animal Bodies
    1-4048-0103-0
Does an Elephant Fit in Your Hand? A Book About Animal Sizes
    1-4048-2235-6